WORLD ECONOMY

What's the Future?

Matt Anniss

Gareth Stevens
Publishing

Please visit our website, www.garethstevens.com. For a free color catalog of all our high-quality books, call toll free 1-800-542-2595 or fax 1-877-542-2596.

Library of Congress Cataloging-in-Publication Data

Anniss, Matt.
 World economy : what's the future? / Matt Anniss.
    p. cm. — (Ask the experts)
 Includes index.
ISBN 978-1-4339-8648-2 (pbk.)
ISBN 978-1-4339-8649-9 (6-pack)
ISBN 978-1-4339-8647-5 (library binding)
1. Economic history—21st century. 2. Economic forecasting. 3. Global Financial Crisis, 2008-2009. I. Title.
 HC59.3.A56 2013
 330.9—dc23

2012037833

First Edition

Published in 2013 by
Gareth Stevens Publishing
111 East 14th Street, Suite 349
New York, NY 10003

© 2013 Gareth Stevens Publishing

Produced by Calcium, www.calciumcreative.co.uk
Designed by Emma DeBanks and Paul Myerscough
Edited by Sarah Eason

Photo credits: Dreamstime: 1000words 12, Americanspirit 30, Blacjack 15, Dublinuser 14, Jborzicchi 21, Joaobambu 23, Kpikoulas 38, Miker75 28, Paura 22, Pinkcandy 32, Robcorbett cover (c), 35, Seast 20, Sigurdurwilliam 10, Springdt313 19, Szirtesi 33, Tdmartin 29, Vacclav 34, Vagrant83 31; Istockphoto: Mario Tama 5; Shutterstock: Arindambanerjee 17, Chaoss 41, Creativei Images 24, Ioana Davies 26, Fatseyeva 1, 16, Goodluz 40, Bianda Ahmad Hisham cover (b), Sergej Khakimullin cover (t), Kuzma 7, Daryl Lang 27, 42, 43, Rafael Ramirez Lee 37, Lisa S. 45, Losevsky Photo and Video 25, Michael Jung 11, Tan Wei Ming 4, Monkey Business Images 8, P Cruciatti 18, 44, Portokalis 13, Vasily Smirnov 36, Albert H. Teich 9, Yurchyks 39.

Printed in the United States of America

CPSIA compliance information: Batch #CW13GS: For further information contact Gareth Stevens, New York, New York at 1-800-542-2595.

Contents

Open up a newspaper or turn on a television news channel, and you will find gloomy headlines about money matters around the world. They say that the world economy is in bad shape, we are in a deep recession, and the future looks uncertain. What is the economy, and why are the media predictions so bleak?

An Uncertain Future

The economy is what experts call the system by which money is created, exchanged, and moved around a country and, in turn, around the world. When times are good, there is a lot of money in the system, which makes people more likely to buy and sell things. This creates more jobs, and even more money.

Face Facts

"As sure as the spring will follow the winter, prosperity and economic growth will follow recession."
Bo Bennett, Internet millionaire

Some countries, such as China, are still enjoying a booming economy despite the recession elsewhere.

The world economy has been in turmoil ever since the failure of the banking system in 2008.

GOING DOWN

Right now, times are bad and the state of the US economy, and of the world economy, is weak. There is less money in the system, fewer jobs, and people are spending less. When an economy is weak, it is said to be in recession. According to most experts, the world economy is currently in the middle of a very bad recession.

EXPERT OPINION

In this book, we will look in detail at the future of the world economy, asking whether things are going to get better or worse in the years ahead. We will also look at the way some economies around the world are booming, while many European countries and the United States are struggling.

ask the experts

Most experts agree that the current economic crisis is the worst since the Great Depression in the 1930s, when millions of Americans lost their jobs and homes. There is disagreement over just how bad things are, though. Some say the current recession will last another 10 years, while others think it will be over soon. Who is right?

Recession is not a new thing. Throughout history, the fortunes of countries have risen and fallen in line with their economies. Experts call this "boom and bust." Right now, many countries, including the United States, are in recession. So how did this happen?

Crash and Burn

During the 1990s and early 2000s, many countries enjoyed a "boom" period. Credit, which means people can borrow money and pay it back later, was more easily available than ever before. People did not worry about paying off their loans—times were good and life was easy.

Protests about the current poor state of the economy are becoming a regular sight on our streets.

BANKER ATE ALL THE PIES

Face Facts

"The world has been spending staggering amounts of money that it doesn't have for a few decades now, and it's all coming home to roost."
Jim Rogers, international investment banker

6

When the economy crashes, some people lose their homes and are forced to sleep on the streets.

All Fall Down

In the fall of 2007, our money systems started to unravel. In the United States, a number of banks began to lose money quickly, as it became clear that they had lent money to people who could not pay them back. Within a year, the crisis had spread worldwide. Very quickly, governments had to step in to save the banks from running out of money.

Downturn

Since then, things have gone from bad to worse. People have lost their jobs and with it their homes, which they bought with loans from banks that were close to collapse. Most people have a lot less money now and many do not have any spare money for luxuries or vacations.

"the debate

Experts disagree on how to make the economy strong again. Some think that the way to improve the economy is to make it easier for companies to create jobs for people. Other experts disagree. They say that the only way forward is to "stimulate" economic activity by pumping more money into the system."

No Way Back?

The health of the world economy is based on people creating, earning, and spending money. Until people have more money, they cannot spend it. But until people spend more money, the economy will not recover. Governments need to find ways to create more jobs and make people wealthier. Then they will start buying goods once more.

GAMBLING WITH OUR FUTURE

Many experts say that the current recession can be blamed on the banks. They say that the banks did not carry out enough checks before they lent money to companies, governments, and individuals. When people and organizations could not pay back the money they owed, the banks became short of money and the economy failed.

EASY COME, EASY GO

In the years leading up to the economic crash in 2008, many banks in the United States and Europe lent money to people so that they could buy their own homes. The banks made money by charging people interest to borrow money from them. However, many of these people could not afford to repay their loans, but the banks still lent them the money. These loans became bad debts. When the banks realized they were unlikely to get their money back, many sold on the debts to other banks around the world. The problem then got bigger as more and more banks owned bad debts, which became known as "toxic debts."

Face Facts

"Time is running out fast. I think we maybe have a few months—it could be weeks, it could be days—before financial catastrophe." Willem Buiter, chief economist, Citigroup, November, 2011

When it became clear that the banks were in trouble, stockbrokers lost confidence in the economy and panic set in worldwide.

8

Ben Bernanke of the US Federal Reserve agreed to loan US banks billions of dollars to stop them from collapsing.

HOUSE OF CARDS

In 2008, it was the collapse of a large international bank called Lehman Brothers that set off the current economic crisis. Many smaller banks around the world were dependent on Lehman Brothers. Once the large bank closed, the smaller banks ran out of money. Others were saved from the brink of closure by money from national governments. In order to hold onto the money they did have, banks stopped lending money to businesses and individuals, even to those who could afford to pay it back. A healthy economy needs the banks to lend to these people, so they can start new businesses and other ventures. Without it, money stops passing through the system and the economy falls into recession.

CASINO BANKING

Since the crisis, many banks have recovered and are now making money again. Experts say that the banks were unprofessional and gambled with our money—they might be recovering, but our economies certainly are not.

9

Many people in countries such as Greece have protested about the government cuts to their public services.

The Debt Crisis

The biggest single problem currently affecting the world economy is debt. Individuals, companies, and governments around the world have many debts. The level of debt has been rising for decades. Many experts think that it was a reliance on borrowing too much money that caused the economy to crash in 2008. The question now is how can we repay the huge sums of money that we owe?

ask the experts

Experts agree that sovereign debt is one of the greatest problems facing the world right now. Sovereign debt is the total amount of money owed by each country. Experts say that if we do not create ways to boost the economy, many countries could run out of money in the next 20 years. If this happens, another severe world crisis would occur.

GOVERNMENT BORROWING

Many governments around the world are deeply in debt. This is because they have borrowed money to pay for public services, such as building schools or hospitals, or to buy weapons for wars. Whatever the reason, many nations now owe vast sums that they may struggle to pay back in the future.

The amount of money owed by nations is staggering. The United States has more than $5 trillion worth of debt, according to current statistics, while the United Kingdom owes more than £66 billion. The total amount of "sovereign debt" currently stands at $45 trillion. Many believe this debt is unsustainable.

TROUBLE AHEAD?

When times are good and there is a lot of money in the economy, sovereign debt is not a problem because governments can easily meet the payments they must make on these loans. However, when times are bad, it can become an enormous problem.

To pay their debts, governments must either spend less money by cutting public services, or raise more money by increasing the taxes people pay. These policies make it harder for the country's economy to grow. The policies are also unpopular with ordinary people, who are taxed to raise money and who lose out when public services are cut.

Face Facts

"Today we spend more on paying back debts than we do on running schools. For every single pound Britons pay in tax, 10 pence is spent on debt repayment."
David Cameron,
British Prime Minister.

Many people have used credit cards to buy goods, leading to big debts that they cannot afford to repay.

TROUBLE BREWING

When the world economy crashes, it is not just a lack of money in the system we have to worry about. Often, the issues caused by a broken economy—a lack of jobs, mass poverty, and people losing their homes—can trigger huge problems in society such as crime, riots, and even the fall of governments.

PEACEFUL PROTESTS

When people see themselves becoming poorer as a result of a failing economy, it makes them angry. Sometimes people express their anger through peaceful protests, such as marches or demonstrations. In 2011 and 2012, the "Occupy" movement around the world was an example of this anger. People set up camps in high-profile locations to express their views and outrage.

Anger is growing around the world at the way governments are handling the current crisis in the economy.

Face Facts

"The choice we face is one of sacrifice or even greater sacrifice—on a scale that cannot be compared."
Evangelos Venizelos, Finance Minister, Greece

Violence on the Streets

If a government is forced to make extreme cuts, it increases the likelihood that angry and frustrated people will turn to violence. Since 2010, Greece has been torn apart by rioting on the streets resulting from the country's huge economic problems. The Greek government had to ask other European nations to lend them more than $110 billion, to prevent their country's economy from falling apart.

Austerity Measures

To obtain the money, the Greek government had to agree to introduce severe "austerity measures" in their country. This meant that the government had to spend less on services but still had to raise even more taxes to pay off its huge debts.

Greece has seen both peaceful and violent protests against government action taken to deal with its financial crisis.

ask the experts

Many experts say that what has happened in Greece is a warning to other nations in trouble. They say there is a strong chance that trouble like this could spread to other parts of the world if the economy does not recover soon. However, most agree that unpopular austerity measures are essential to solve the economic problems in countries such as Greece.

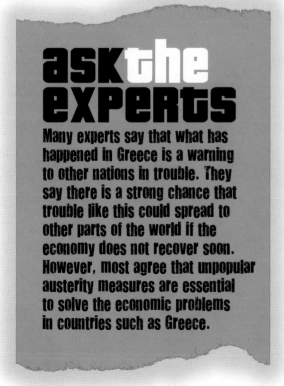

Anger Turns to Protest

The austerity policies were extremely unpopular, because they made most people much poorer. Many people in Greece felt their government was responsible for getting them into such enormous debt. The people felt they were suffering because of the mistakes of both the bankers and the government. Soon, some people's anger turned to protests on the streets.

The Comeback Kids

Over the last 15 years, a number of countries have run out of money to pay off their many debts and have been declared "bankrupt." This means they were unable to pay their debt. Now, many of these countries are booming, with strong economies. They are the world economy's "comeback kids."

Going Bust

In 2001, Argentina was engulfed in a massive crisis when its economy collapsed. Members of the public, worried about losing their savings, lined up all night outside banks to take out their money. Faced with debts of more than $145 billion, Argentina's president was forced to announce to the world that his country had gone bust.

ASK the EXPERTS

Some experts think that allowing countries to go bust and start again is the only way to deal with their dying economies, whatever the consequences. This is a risky move, as it could cause greater problems elsewhere in the world, but it is one that some countries may soon have no choice but to make.

Could Ireland make a comeback? Its business taxes are at a record low to attract investers such as Google in order to boost its economy.

14

The German chancellor Angela Merkel is leading EU talks to try to stop failing European economies from going bust.

Growing Economy

In 2002, a new government was elected. They put money into public services to make sure that people could survive the crisis. They also cut taxes and encouraged businesses to grow. Soon, countries around the world were buying more Argentine products, such as soy and beef, and the economy quickly recovered. Today, Argentina is thriving and has one of the fastest growing economies in the world.

Face Facts

"The best way to avoid a bust is to avoid having an unsustainable boom in the first place. Unfortunately, that's a lesson that none of us seems to learn."
Matthew Partridge, business journalist

Fighting Back

In 2008, Iceland suffered similar problems to Argentina. Yet between 2010 and 2012, the country's economy grew rapidly. A similar thing may happen to Ireland, a country that just escaped going bust in 2008. The government lowered taxes to attract outside investment from businesses such as Google, and hopes are that the economy will bounce back as a result.

It is not all doom and gloom around the world. While countries with traditionally strong economies such as the United States, the United Kingdom, France, and Spain have recently been in decline, other nations have seen their fortunes rise. Countries whose economies were not closely linked to the banking system were able to ride out the storm and emerge stronger.

A New World Order

The United Arab Emirates is an oil-rich country that has not been affected by the global economic crisis.

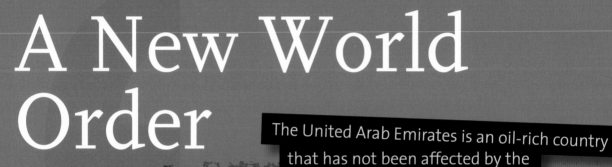

Face Facts

"It is realistic to say that within 10 years, China's economy will be roughly the same size as the US economy."
Tom Miller, economist, GK Dragonomics

Many computer firms have opened up factories in China and India, where making products is cheaper.

DEVELOPING POWERS

Many of the world's fastest-growing economies are in Asia, the Middle East, and South America. These are places that, until recently, did not have the systems or structures in place to compete with the United States and Europe. Now they do, and they want to use this advantage to transform themselves into economic superpowers.

CHANGING TIMES

Experts think that this could be the first stage of a "new world order," with new economic superpowers leading the world forward. Soon, it may be China, India, Saudi Arabia, and Brazil calling the shots, not the United States and Europe. It may take a while, but the developing world may one day dominate the world economy.

ask the experts

Experts agree that although there are many countries with the potential to become new "economic superpowers," this will not happen overnight. They say that it will take at least a decade for China to overtake the United States as the world's biggest economy, and many more for India and other developing nations to compete.

17

Unstoppable China?

In 2011, the economies of Asian countries were responsible for more than one-quarter of the world's total goods and services. Leading the charge was China. In 2011 alone, the Chinese economy grew by 10 percent. This meant that the country was hundreds of billions of dollars richer than it was the year before. Most experts say that China will overtake the United States as the world's biggest single economy by 2020. One expert, Anvind Subramanian, says the country already has, and that the change took place in 2010. Whoever you believe, China is fast becoming the world's number one economic force.

"the debate

Can China's economy keep growing as fast as it has in recent years? Some experts think that over the next 30 years, China's economy will stop growing as other nations catch up. Others say that the opposite will happen, and it will continue to grow as demand for products increases worldwide. "

Today, China has a thriving economy that threatens to topple the great economic superpowers in the West.

Face Facts

"China was top dog economically for thousands of years. In some ways, the past few hundred years have just been a blip."
Anvind Subramanian, economist and writer

THE WORLD'S FACTORY

It costs less to make things in China than in the United States or Europe. This is mostly because workers' wages are lower there. Because of this, many companies are setting up factories in China. Now, everything from iPods and computers, to clothes and sneakers, are made in China. In 2011, more than $181 billion worth of products were exported from China to be sold overseas.

CHEAP LABOR

Another factor in China's rise is the number of people who live in the country. It has a population of more than 1.2 billion. That's a lot of people who can work in factories, for lower wages, in order for people in the West to buy cheap cell phones and televisions.

It is almost impossible for the United States and Europe to compete with China. Most people in the West demand much higher wages to do the same job a worker in China will do for far less money. It costs the West more to produce goods, and most countries simply cannot compete with China.

The Indian Boom

In many ways, the transformation of India from a developing country into a new economic superpower has been even more amazing than that of China. The country's economy is now six times bigger than it was 20 years ago. That is a remarkable turnaround. Some experts now think that the Indian economy is the third biggest in the world.

Low Wages

Like China, India has profited from offering its services to the world. Also like China, products can be made very cheaply in India. This is because most Indian workers are paid much lower wages than their American counterparts. Another advantage the country has is that it can build factories in which to make goods very cheaply.

Experts argue that India's population is so enormous that many will remain poor and jobless, despite the booming economy.

Face Facts

"From 2007 to 2020, India's economy will grow four times in size. By 2043, it will be bigger than the United States."
Tushar Poddar, economist, Goldman Sachs

India's automobile industry is one of the fastest growing in the world, thanks to the country's huge demand for cars.

BOOM SECTORS

Although India still does not make as many products as China, some industries are booming. For example, many international drug companies now choose to make their pills and medicines in factories in the country. Another booming industry in India is clothing manufacturing. Currently, more than 20 percent of the country's workforce is employed making clothes.

CALL CENTERS

Another rapid area of expansion in India has been the country's service industry. The official language of India is English, and many English-speaking people are employed in telephone call centers.

ask the experts

Most experts agree that India's economy will continue growing quickly in the coming years. However, many experts think that India has to spend more money on its infrastructure, including highways, ports, and airports, if it wants its booming economy to continue to grow at the same rate.

Companies in the United States and the United Kingdom use call centers to offer customer services, such as advice and assistance, to their customers. It is cheaper to employ people in India to do this than it would be "back home." Workers will also work at night, so companies can offer a 24-hour service.

The Brazilian Boom

As the largest country in South America, Brazil has always been thought of as an economic superpower in waiting. Now, thanks to a huge boom in business in the last decade, Brazil has one of the fastest-growing economies in the world.

Carnival of Business

Like other developing nations on the rise, Brazil's economy is getting bigger every year. It is now the sixth largest economy in the world, and is predicted to be the fifth largest by the middle of 2013. Brazil is a vast country, with lots of natural resources such as farmland, oil, and gas. This means it is in a very strong position to continue growing.

ask the experts

Despite huge growth in recent years, experts say that Brazil's economy may not be as strong as previously thought. Although many still believe that the country will become the world's fourth biggest economy by 2050, some say statistics show that Brazil could fall into recession by the middle of 2013.

Experts hope that the country's booming economy will lift many of its people out of poverty.

Face Facts

"...with huge amounts of natural resources, including oil and gas, Brazil is very well placed for the future."
Francisco Itzaina,
Chief Executive,
Rolls-Royce Brazil

Brazil has devoted vast amounts of land to cattle farming to feed its huge beef export market.

An Export Boom

Brazil's boom has been driven by an increase in exports, which are goods produced and sold to other countries. Brazil is the world's biggest producer of iron. It also exports more beef, chicken, orange juice, sugar, coffee, and tobacco than any other nation on Earth. The country is also the home of the world's largest aircraft maker, Embraer.

Clever Deals

Brazil has been clever in who it chooses to do business with. China is its biggest trade partner, and much of the food and drink Brazil produces goes to Asia. And as China is the largest nation on Earth, it is unlikely that orders to Brazil will dry up in the near future. If anything, Brazil will have to increase its production output to satisfy the levels of demand in its Asian markets.

23

PetroDollars

Although they are relatively small in size, a handful of countries in the Middle East are fast becoming some of the most important players on the global economic scene. Their extreme wealth, which is based on sales of oil and gas, is now being used to invest in building projects and to buy businesses around the world.

Oil Rich

The Middle East produces more oil and gas than anywhere else on Earth. These are the two most precious natural resources in the world. The business of extracting and selling these resources has made a handful of sheiks, the traditional rulers of Arab countries, very rich indeed. As a result, their countries are also very wealthy.

Some wealthy Arab states have invested in spectacular building projects, such as this one in Abu Dhabi.

Face Facts

"Control over the production and distribution of oil is the decisive factor in defining who rules the Middle East."
Christopher Hitchens, journalist

Middle East nations such as the United Arab Emirates and Saudi Arabia have made their wealth through oil export.

Small Country, Strong and Growing Economy

One of the most remarkable nations of the Middle East is the United Arab Emirates. The country is home to just 8 million people, but it has the 30th largest economy in the world. In recent years, the price of oil has increased as supplies have become much scarcer around the world. Because of this, the economy of the United Arab Emirates is growing in size year after year.

Wise Spenders

The rulers of the United Arab Emirates have used the extra money in their economy wisely. As well as spending billions of dollars on building hotels in their two biggest cities, Dubai and Abu Dhabi, they have also set themselves up as an alternative to traditional banks. Over the last 10 years, they have lent money to other countries and invested almost $400 billion in lucrative building projects around the world.

ask the experts

Experts say that the growth of Middle Eastern economies could slow down in future years unless they create more jobs. According to a group of experts, Arab countries will need to create 75 million extra jobs for young people in the next 10 years, just to keep people employed and prevent poverty in sections of the population.

The aftershocks of the 2008 banking crisis are still being felt around the world. While China, India, and other fast-rising economic superpowers-in-waiting are forging ahead, the United States and Europe continue to struggle, weighed down by billions of dollars of debts. Is this the beginning of the end for these countries, or just another blip on the radar?

Go West

Wall Street in New York is the center of the financial services industry in the United States. Will it be the center of the world economy in the future?

ASK the EXPERTS

Many experts think that the economies of the Western powers could take up to 20 years to recover from the 2008 crisis. They point to what happened in Japan in the 1990s, when a "lost decade" followed a severe economic crash. If experts are right, many Western countries could experience a "lost decade" of their own.

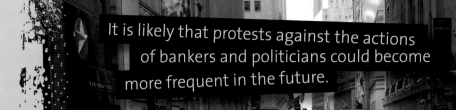

It is likely that protests against the actions of bankers and politicians could become more frequent in the future.

Ever Changing

The economy is a complicated system. It changes all the time as stock markets, in which money and shares in companies are bought and sold, rise and fall again. Economists have many conflicting ideas about how best to achieve a successful economy. At present, most simply do not agree on the best way forward.

Conflicting Ideas

Some economists think that the basis of a strong economy lies in making and selling goods to other countries. This is called exporting. Others think that the key to success lies in building strong banks and financial services. These sections of the economy are the businesses that buy and sell money and shares in companies.

Face Facts

"As debt levels get bigger and bigger, eventually you get to the point where the recovery stalls because you haven't dealt with your debts."
Karen Ward, economist, HSBC Bank

Confusion

Right now, nobody knows what the future holds. In the past, the traditional Western powers, led by the United States, developed strong banking and financial services in their economies. When those industries collapsed in 2008, it brought our economy to the brink of destruction. So, where do we go next, and will our economies ever recover from the financial crisis?

Some Americans think that the government has ruined the economy, and only radical change will save it from collapse.

Face Facts

"Economic growth without social progress lets the great majority of people remain in poverty, while a few reap the benefits."
John F. Kennedy, US President 1961–63

THE UNITED STATES IN DECLINE?

The United States of America is the world's original economic superpower. Since the end of the British Empire in the mid-twentieth century, the United States has been the leader on the world stage. With China and India following close behind, the country now faces a fight to remain the number one economy.

IN RECESSION

Since the economic crash of 2008, the United States has felt the effects of a deep recession. Many companies have closed, leaving millions of people without jobs. In the summer of 2010, one in 10 American adults was out of work—that's about 10 percent of the working population. This has since fallen to 8 percent, but there are still more than 12 million Americans without a job today.

Easing Answer?

President Obama has tried to end the recession by pumping hundreds of billions of dollars into the economy in a process called "quantitative easing." The money was given to banks so that they would lend it to businesses. The hope was that these businesses would create many new jobs. Unfortunately, so far this strategy has not worked.

Gloomy Outlook

If the US economy continues in recession, it will soon lose its position as the world's biggest economy. The government is trying to kick-start the economy, but it is proving very difficult to do. Experts warn that if the economy does not pick up soon, the country could slip into a permanent decline.

"the debate

Experts disagree about what the United States should be doing to address its problems. Some people think that the only way to get the economy going again is to cut taxes, so that people have more money in their pocket to spend on goods and services. Other experts disagree. They say that the way to fix the economy is to encourage businesses to create more jobs. If more people are working, they have money to spend on goods and services. Furthermore, if they are employed in making goods, the goods can be exported around the world. "

Since the 2008 banking crisis, President Obama has tried many strategies to try to grow the economy.

A United States Debt Crisis?

One of the biggest problems faced by the United States is its level of debt. The US government currently owes more than $15 trillion. Experts say that by 2015, the government could be spending $700 billion a year on debt repayments. Is the government storing up problems for future generations?

Interest Explained

If you take a loan from a bank, you have to pay back the money over a certain period of time. An extra amount is added to the amount you originally borrowed. This is called interest. The interest is a percentage of the total amount you borrow. The longer you take to pay off the loan, the more interest you have to pay. Since the US government owes so much money, its interest payments could be more than $4.2 trillion over the next decade.

Stabilizing the economy after the 2008 Wall Street crash has left the US government trillions of dollars in debt.

ask the experts

Experts agree that the debts of the United States are a big problem, but they disagree about how much of a problem this is. Some economists believe that the government should be doing more to address the problem now, before it is too late. Others are not as concerned.

Many Americans are angry about the way the government has handled the economy over the last few years.

PAY NOW, BUY LATER

Many experts believe that the US government should pay off more of its debt. To do this, the government would have to find much more money, either by raising taxes or by cutting the amount it spends. However, if it does this, it risks weakening the economy even more. If people have less money, they cannot boost the economy by buying things. It is a delicate balance.

AN IMPORTANT TIME

The way the US economy develops over the next few years could shape the country's future. If the economy improves, the government will earn more in taxes and will pay off more of the debt. If it does not improve, things could get a lot worse for ordinary people, and the country's debts could pull it even farther into trouble.

The End of the European Dream?

The problems facing the United States are nothing compared to the ones faced by countries inside the European Union. There, many countries including Spain, Portugal, Italy, and Greece, are teetering on the edge of economic collapse.

Eurozone Problems

Seventeen countries in Europe share a currency, known as the euro (the European equivalent of the dollar). These are called the eurozone countries. Because all these countries use the same currency, their financial problems are shared. That means that if the economy of just one of the eurozone countries collapses, its failure could put the whole eurozone at risk.

A Worsening Crisis

Many eurozone countries are struggling with high levels of national debt. As the recession caused by the 2008 banking crash has deepened, some countries have been unable to make their huge debt repayments. To date, the European Central Bank, led by Germany, has had to "bail out" Greece, Ireland, and Portugal to stop their economies from collapsing. This means the Central Bank has given these countries many billions of euros.

The nations within the eurozone are struggling to bring a huge economic crisis under control.

Face Facts

"Europe could muddle through, but the risk is rising. There could be a catastrophic moment if the crisis is not handled properly." Robert Zoellick, Chairman, World Bank

BAD NEWS

Experts fear that more countries could follow, with Spain and Italy in real danger. There is a real possibility that the whole eurozone could collapse at some point in the next few years, leading to a deep recession all over Europe. This could have a serious impact on the world economy.

When the Greek economy collapsed, the bulding industry collapsed too, leaving many new buildings half finished.

VILLAS FOR SAL
ΠΟΛΕΙΤΑΙ
TEL
9·00 AM –1·
6·00 PM –11

ask the experts

Experts believe that if the eurozone failed, it could take many other economies, including that of the United States, with it. They say that because so many countries around the world trade with countries in the eurozone, the effects of any crash would be felt all over the planet. The world could be plunged into the biggest economic crisis for centuries, and one far worse than the crisis of 2008.

THE LESSONS OF HISTORY

Experts say that the current recession has the potential to be the worst the world has ever seen. However, it is by no means the first. Throughout the last 100 years, the world economy has been hit by many recessions and recovered. So, what can we learn from the economic disasters of the past?

BOOM AND BUST

Most recessions happen after a period of quick economic growth. Eventually, the economy gets too big and the prices of shares in companies fall dramatically.

This triggers a collapse. The worst recession ever seen was the Great Depression of the 1930s. It was triggered by the stock exchange crash on Wall Street in October 1929.

Face Facts

"My daughter asked me, 'What's the economic crisis?' and I said, 'It's something that happens every five to seven years.'"
Jamie Dimon, Chief Executive, JP Morgan

This statue commemorates the victims of the Great Depression. Millions of people were made homeless and hungry by the crisis.

ask the experts

Many experts believe that recessions, however painful, are an inevitable consequence of the way our economy works. They say that any economy cannot continue growing forever. At some point it will weaken and crash. They call this "boom and bust." Right now, we are in a bust period. One day, the economy will boom again.

Some protesters fear that the current recession could be worse and longer-lasting than the Great Depression of the 1930s.

THE WORST RECESSION

The Great Depression had a crippling effect on the United States, and many other countries around the world. At one point, one-quarter of all American adults were without work. All trade between countries was cut in half. Eventually, the world economy grew again, but it took many years for the system to recover.

HISTORY REPEATING

The 1980s were another period of great economic growth around the world. That came to a shuddering halt in 1987, with another Wall Street crash. It was so bad that the leading companies in the United States lost almost one-quarter of their value. It took until the late 1990s for the world economy to fully recover.

Some experts believe that making more goods in the United States and selling them abroad is the quickest way to solve our economic problems.

Face Facts

"Are we on a path not only of crises, but also of crises of increasing frequency and rising severity?"
Fred Bergsten, Petersen Institute for International Economics

What does the future hold for the world economy? In banks and boardrooms all around the world, economists and other experts are asking themselves the same question. What are the economic challenges facing our leaders and our money experts over the next few years?

Into the Future

Our most pressing problem is national debt. This problem could see the International Monetary Fund (IMF) and the World Bank play a bigger role in the world economy. These two organizations lend money to governments when they are in crisis. However, both of them are funded by payments from governments. If governments fail to pay back their loans, could even these banks eventually run out of money?

Hack at It

There is another potential problem facing the world economy. When criminals attack international computer systems, it is called hacking. Today, most trade, business, and banking is done using computers. Could computer hackers bring down the economy?

Can't Agree

We also have to deal with the politics of the economic situation. Our politicians rarely agree on what is best for the economy, and it is the same around the world. The decisions politicians make now could affect the economy for many years to come. If the world economy continues to struggle, we could see an enormous rise in extreme governments. And their ideas about how to deal with the economic crisis will be radical.

A mass organized attack by computer hackers could rob banks of billions of dollars, leaving our accounts empty.

ask the experts

Economists agree that we are facing a long period of uncertainty, as gradual changes in the world economy begin to take effect. They all say that governments in the United States and Europe must act quickly to address their problems. Failure to act now could lead to even greater disaster in the future.

How Deep Are Our Pockets?

The global economy is supported by two organizations founded in 1944, toward the end of World War II. They are the IMF and the World Bank. These institutions exist to prevent global economic meltdown. In the years to come, they will play a huge role in the economic affairs of countries worldwide.

How the IMF Works

The IMF gets its money directly from its members, namely the countries of the world. Each country must pay a certain amount to the IMF each year, depending on how wealthy it is.

The richest countries pay the most, and the poorest pay the least. The IMF holds the money in its central reserves, ready to use in the event of an economic crisis.

Face Facts

"The world is governed by institutions that are not democratic: the World Bank, the IMF, and the World Trade Organization."
Jose Sarrango,
Nobel Prize winner

Some protesters have accused the IMF of being undemocratic, and working to further the interests of the United States and Europe.

LENDING A HAND

If a country gets into trouble, it can apply to the IMF for a loan. Since 1991, the amount loaned by the IMF to countries in trouble has increased by one-fifth. That means that richer countries have had to pay higher amounts into the IMF. Now that some of the world's wealthiest countries are struggling economically, that could spell real problems for the IMF. Its donors may not be able to make their payments.

TROUBLE BREWING?

Another potential issue is how the IMF is run. At present, the richest countries have the biggest say in how decisions are made. That means that the United States wields the most power. However, some experts think that the United States will soon be overtaken by China, India, and Brazil in economic power.

New economic powers such as China might have different views about the how the IMF should do business, and which countries it should lend money to. This change in world power could mean danger for an already fragile world economy.

If the current economic crisis deepens, the IMF may have to help many European nations.

ask the experts

Some experts have criticized the IMF. Some have accused it of favoring the wealthy nations, while others say that it can cause more problems than it solves. Many experts think that Argentina's huge monthly loan repayments to the IMF caused it to run out of money in 2001. Could exactly the same situation now happen in Europe, too?

Face Facts

We now pay for most things using our phones or computers, which can increase the risk of our money being stolen by computer hackers.

The Digital Economy

In times gone by, all banking and trade was done with "real money." Coins, banknotes, and checks (written notes used to tell banks to pay an amount from one person to another) were exchanged. Now, almost all trade and banking is carried out on computers. Some experts think that this could lead to the downfall of the world economy.

Big Weakness

Our reliance on using computers to keep track of money could be our greatest weakness. It leaves us open to attack by gangs of computer hackers, experts in computer systems who want to steal vast sums of money. Experts call these people "cyber criminals." A few isolated attacks are not enough to damage the economy severely. However, if hackers organized one huge, global attack, it could mean disaster.

CYBER ATTACKS

Governments around the world are worried about the possibility of a devastating attack by cyber criminals. They are spending huge amounts of money trying to make their computer systems safe against hacking attacks. If cyber criminals broke into their computer systems, they could steal billions of dollars in seconds.

ENEMY ACTION

Some governments think that spies from other countries are trying to hack into their computers to steal money. They call this "economic espionage." If a country succeeded in weakening another's economy using hacking, it would give it a huge advantage. Hacking could be more effective than war in destroying an enemy country.

Many now question the safety of our banking sytems. Could technology turn out to be our greatest enemy?

ask the experts

Many experts say that attacks from cyber criminals and enemy spies are a huge threat to our economy. In 2011, the British government said that it had fended off cyber-attacks against its computer systems from China and North Korea. US government representatives say that their computer systems have also been attacked by hackers.

Some people are angry at bankers for causing the economic crisis, and believe that we would be better off if the government controlled our banks.

The Politics of Money

The economy has always been at the heart of politics. Over the last 100 years, the conflicts between politicians with different opinions on how a country's economy should be run has shaped the way we live our lives, how much money is in our pockets, and even our future.

Capitalism and Socialism

Most countries in the world base their economy on the principles of what is known as capitalism. That broadly means allowing free trade between people and nations. The economy is driven by the supply of and demand for goods and services. Some countries around the world reject this idea in favor of an idea called socialism. This aims to distribute money more equally amongst everyone in society. The distribution of wealth is controlled centrally by the country's government.

"the debate

The arguments between capitalists and socialists continue to shape the world we live in. Socialists still believe that isolationism will fix their economy, and make things better for the poor. However, capitalists argue that restricting free trade around the world will harm the economy and make things worse.

When times are hard and people are poorer, many people campaign for political change.

RISE OF THE ISOLATIONISTS

When the economy crashes and times are hard, it increases the likelihood that countries will turn to "isolationism." This is when a country restricts the amount of goods it allows to be bought in, or imported, from elsewhere in the world. Instead of buying goods from other countries, a country promotes the buying of products made at home. This ensures that the money people spend does not leave the country, so stays within its economy.

A CHANGING WORLD

Isolationism and socialism are more likely to appeal to people in times of hardship, because they think these policies will improve their lives. They are less likely to consider the wider question of the health of the world economy. Experts warn that if the current economic situation does not improve soon, we could see a rise in isolationism around the world.

Face Facts

"Economic isolationism is the wrong way to go. Vibrant, successful, growing economies that advance the interests of their citizens engage the global economy."
John W. Snow, US Secretary of the Treasury, 2003–2006.

43

The world economy is always changing. Every day, our economic prospects change as the world's governments and money markets react to the latest news from home and abroad. Economists change their predictions almost as quickly as they change their clothes. So, what do you think will happen in the future?

You're the Expert

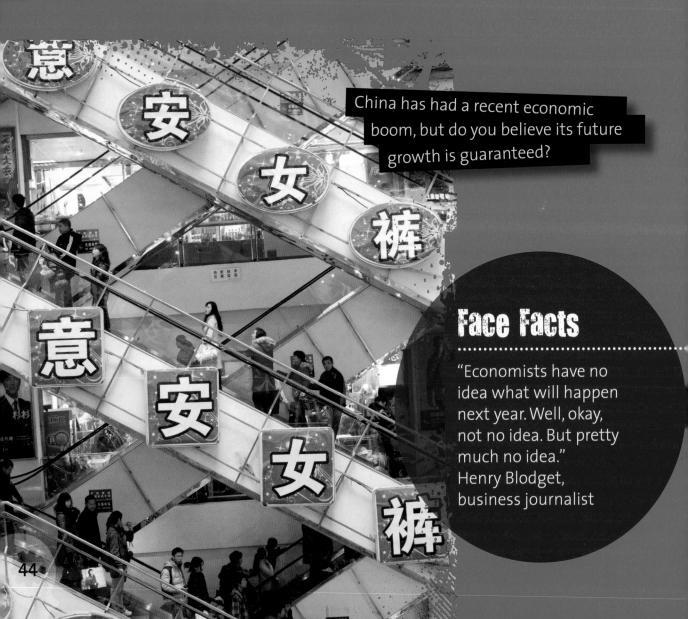

China has had a recent economic boom, but do you believe its future growth is guaranteed?

Face Facts

"Economists have no idea what will happen next year. Well, okay, not no idea. But pretty much no idea."
Henry Blodget, business journalist

Big Questions

So what do you think will happen to the world economy in coming years? Will the United States, as some predict, be overtaken by China or India as the world's leading economic superpower? If so, what will this mean for ordinary Americans in years to come? Perhaps you believe that the government will find a way to restore the United States' position as the world's richest country.

Will Debt Destroy Us?

What do you think we should do about the problem of sovereign debt—the money owed by countries to the IMF and others? Will the weight of debt bring down many European countries, or will they find ways to pay it off and guarantee the survival of the eurozone?

Finding the Answers

Your answers will not change the world, but they may help you understand the complicated and often confusing world of economics. Different experts have different views about how best to deal with our economic crisis. If you were the expert, what would you decide?

ask the experts

Economists try to predict the future so that governments and businesses can plan ahead. However, very few get their predictions right. This is because the economy is so complicated and can change in a few hours, days, or weeks. Economists make a calculated guess based on facts, but it is always just a guess.

When it comes to money and economics, nobody can say for sure what will happen in the future.

Glossary

austerity measures government policies in times of economic difficulty, such as cuts to spending on public services and higher taxes

bankrupt legally unable to pay off your debts due to lack of money

capitalism an economic system in which trade is controlled by private owners, and not by the government

catastrophic very bad

crisis a bad situation caused by a big event, such as a war or an economic collapse

currency the type of money used by a country or group of countries, such as the dollar and the euro

debt something owed by one person or country to another

economics the study of economies

economist an expert in the study of economics

economy the flow of money, based on the trading of goods and services

employed having work

European Union (EU) a political and economic union of 27 of the countries in Europe

eurozone a group of 17 countries in Europe that all use the euro as their currency

finance money

financial services banking and other industries that specialize in lending money

interest a charge added on to a loan by the lender, in addition to the sum borrowed

International Monetary Fund (IMF) an organization that lends money to governments, and is funded by 200 countries around the world

isolationism the economic and political idea that a country is better off if it takes care of itself and does not engage with the rest of the world

loan an amount of money given to someone, which they agree to pay back over a period of time

recession a period of time when a country's economy shrinks, instead of growing

repayments money paid to reduce or pay off a debt

socialism an economic system in which the resources of a country are managed and distributed by the government, so that wealth is more equally shared between people

sovereign debt money owed by a country's government

stock exchange a place where large quantities of money, goods, and shares in companies are bought and sold, such as Wall Street in New York City

superpower a country with great wealth and power in the world, such as the United States or China

tax money paid to the government by individuals or organizations

toxic poisonous

trade the buying and selling of things, such as products and services

Books

Bauman, Yoram, and Grady Klein. *The Cartoon Introduction to Economics Volume 1: Microeconomics.* New York, NY: Hill & Wang, 2010.

Gillman, Laura Ann. *Economics: How Economics Works.* Minneapolis, MN: Lerner Publications, 2005.

Orr, Tamara. *A Kid's Guide to the Economy.* Hockessin, DE: Mitchell Lane, 2009.

For More Information

Websites

There is a useful extended glossary of economic terms at the Scholastic website:
www.scholastic.com/browse/article.jsp?id=3750579

Find lots of information on economics at:
www.socialstudiesforkids.com/subjects/economics.htm

The US Treasury has a great website for kids, full of information and games on economics, at:
www.treasurydirect.gov/kids/kids.htm

Publisher's note to educators and parents: Our editors have carefully reviewed these websites to ensure that they are suitable for students. Many websites change frequently, however, and we cannot guarantee that a site's future contents will continue to meet our high standards of quality and educational value. Be advised that students should be closely supervised whenever they access the Internet.

Index